PLANET EARTH

# AMERICAN PRAIRIES

WILLIAM K SMITHEY

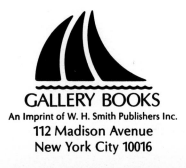

GALLERY BOOKS

An Imprint of W. H. Smith Publishers Inc.

112 Madison Avenue

New York City 10016

**Text**
William K. Smithey

**Editorial**
Gill Waugh

**Design**
Clive Dorman

**Production**
Ruth Arthur
David Proffit
Sally Connolly
Andrew Whitelaw

**Jacket Design**
Claire Leighton

**Commissioning Editor**
Andrew Preston

**Director of Production**
Gerald Hughes

**Publishing Assistant**
Edward Doling

**Director of Publishing**
David Gibbon

**Photography**
Planet Earth Pictures:
J. Brian Alker 7 *bottom*, 9 *bottom*; Franz J. Camenzind 4, 11 *bottom*,
14- 15, 17, 19, 21-23, 27 *bottom*, 31; Mary Clay 6, 9 *top*, 10, 11 *top*, 18
*top*, 20, 25 *top*, 28-30; R. F. Coomber 32; D. Robert Franz 16, 26, 27
*top*; Ken Lucas 13; Dave Lyons 12, 18 *top*; John Lythgoe 7 *top*, 24, 25
*bottom*; David Maitland 5 *top*; Johnathan Scott 5 *bottom*; Nigel
Tucker 8, back cover.
FPG International: R. Cowan front cover.

CLB 2489
This edition published in 1990 by Gallery Books,
an imprint of WH Smith Publishers, Inc,
112 Madison Avenue, New York 10016.
© 1990 Colour Library Books Ltd, Godalming, Surrey, England.
All rights reserved.
Colour separations by Scantrans Pte Ltd, Singapore.
Printed and bound by New Interlitho, Italy.
ISBN 0 8317 6981 5

# CONTENTS

INTRODUCTION 4

WHAT IS SPECIAL ABOUT GRASSES 6

MAN AND THE GREAT PLAINS 7

THE TALLGRASS PRAIRIE 8

THE MIXED PRAIRIE 12

MIXED PRAIRIE WILDLIFE 14

THE SHORTGRASS PRAIRIE 18

PRAIRIE BIRDS 26

PRAIRIE POTHOLES 28

A TALE OF THREE DOGS 30

# INTRODUCTION

The name varies. In South America they are called pampas; in Asia, steppes; in South Africa, the veld. Whatever they call them, all continents except Antarctica contain some type of grassland. In the United States it is the prairie, a vast grassland that stretches west from the Appalachians to the Rocky Mountains.

The term "grass" covers a multiplicity of plants – about 10,000 different species worldwide. Almost without exception, grasses are herbaceous (that is to say they do not form woody tissue), and therefore thrive where woody plants, such as trees and shrubs, cannot. Grasses are masters of adversity, growing in areas where fires are common, where the soil is prohibitively dry or wet, and where grazing animals are abundant.

Throughout the ages, wherever grasslands have flourished, rich collections of grazing and seed-eating animals have evolved. Today, the world's grasslands are home to the most abundant and diverse mammal populations on earth. Australia's kangaroos and wombats, Africa's lions and wildebeest and North America's prairie dogs, bison and pronghorn are but a few of the products of grasslands.

*Below: bison in Yellowstone National Park. Much of the land that supported huge herds of this beast is now used to feed domestic cattle. Marsupials, including the eastern grey kangaroo (facing page top), thrive in the grasslands of Australia. Facing page bottom: herds of wildebeest on the Serengeti, Tanzania.*

# WHAT IS SPECIAL ABOUT GRASSES

Though the flowers are often inconspicuous, all grasses are flowering plants. Much of a grass plant exists under the ground in the form of dense, fibrous root systems and runners called "rhizomes." During the growing season about one-half of the total vegetation of a grassland is below ground. While most plants grow from a region at their tips, grasses grow from the base of their leaves. This is an important distinction, for if the growing tip of a newly-emerged tree seedling is removed by a grazing animal it will usually die. By contrast, in the same circumstances a grass plant will continue to grow, simply manufacturing new leaves.

Because they can sustain growth in the face of environmental calamity, grasslands are enormously productive. While they comprise only about three percent of the earth's total plant matter, grasslands produce nearly five times their share of the new growth in all ecosystems each year. For animals adapted to digest the silica-rich leaves of grasses they form a nutritious diet. Animal evolution has been significantly influenced by this food source ever since the demise of the dinosaur. Thus the rise of mammals is linked to grasslands in a fundamental way.

Grasslands are relatively young environments, having evolved only in the past 100 million years. In the American Midwest, a rich grassland grew in a climate where trees would have flourished if lightning-caused fires had not frequently burned the land. The Midwest resembled the Serengeti; its herds of wild cattle, horses, camels, rhinoceros and elephants preyed upon by wild dogs, large cats and bears.

Many of these ancient grassland species, such as saber-toothed tigers and ground sloths, are now extinct. Others, including rhinoceros, elephants, camels and horses, while thriving elsewhere, have disappeared from North America. The continued drying of the North American climate, combined with the introduction of humans into the Western Hemisphere, are two important reasons. It is clear that humans soon developed into such proficient hunters that they were capable of wiping out entire species.

*Top right: grasses often produce flowers in clusters on tall stems. Because they grow in open, treeless country, grasses (right) rely on the wind to distribute their pollen.*

# MAN AND THE GREAT PLAINS

In the late 1700s, at about the same time as the American Revolution, settlers expanded into the North American interior grasslands. They first encountered the tallgrass prairies of Ohio and Illinois, mistaking their lack of trees as a sign of infertile land.

The tallgrass prairies proved to be among the finest croplands in the world, however. The soil was rich, having been modified by glaciers and mulched and fertilized by thousands of generations of plants and animals. Beneath the sod lay a rich black humus topsoil, as much as five times as rich as forest soil. Once a plow capable of busting through the tough prairie sod had been invented, the Midwest became the United States' breadbasket. Today only a tiny amount of unplowed tallgrass prairie exists, and most of that on rocky, sandy or hilly sites. They lie as remnants of an ecosystem that once covered an area encompassing a dozen states.

*Right: Indian grass is an important part of the tallgrass prairie. In areas of occasional flooding and repeated burning it will form nearly perfect stands. Much of the prairie has been converted to farmland (below).*

# THE TALLGRASS PRAIRIE

Historically, the tallgrass prairie occurred in the Midwest, including much of Iowa, parts of Minnesota, Missouri, and Illinois. It extended west, roughly to the eastern edges of North and South Dakota, Nebraska, Kansas and south into Oklahoma, where it blended in a broad transition zone into the mixed prairies further west. It was the most dramatic of the American grasslands, with grass growing as high as twelve feet. By the turn of the century, because of wholesale conversion to agricultural crops, little of the tallgrass prairie remained.

The western boundary between the tallgrass and mixed prairie errs little from the ninety-eighth meridian of longitude. This cut-off line of the tallgrass prairie essentially reflects a decrease in availability of moisture. Beyond this line, the decrease in precipitation, combined with the increase in evaporation, results in soil moisture insufficient to sustain tallgrass prairie plant species. Precipitation in the tallgrass prairies ranges from twenty-five to about forty inches per year, with more than half of this falling during the spring and summer growing season. Characteristic of many grassland climates is an extreme variability in precipitation from year to year, with drought a frequent occurrence.

Seen in the spring, the tallgrass prairie boasts a great variety of wildflowers as well as many different types of grass. However, the bulk of the vegetation belongs to just a few species, all of which are grasses. Cool-season grasses, such as needlegrass and junegrass, emerge early in the spring before they are shaded out by the taller grasses later in the year. As the growing season progresses, big bluestem becomes the dominant species, its flower stems reaching lengths of up to twelve feet. Prairie cordgrass, which dominates land that is too wet for big bluestem, is one of the tallest and densest prairie grasses, also growing up to twelve feet high in luxuriant stands.

Though grasses dominate, other groups are interspersed amongst them. Two groups are prevalent; legumes, commonly known as the pea family, and composites, colorful sunflowers and goldenrods. Trees, including ash and boxelder, grow mainly along streams, while the bur oak is the most widespread upland prairie tree.

*Below: spring in the Konza tallgrass prairie of Kansas. Only in terrain unsuitable for farming does any of the original tallgrass prairie remain.*

# THE ROLE OF FIRE

The plants that define the tallgrass prairie owe their dominance to fire. Even the impressive prairie fires described by early travelers, extensive enough to allow travel at night and even to read by at a considerable distance, would have left the portion of the grass plant under the ground unaffected. By recycling nutrients and removing debris, fires actually improve grass growth. Furthermore, without periodic scorching the forest would eventually triumph over the grassland. Indeed, as the land was converted to agriculture and attempts were made to control fires, trees successfully took over unburned areas.

The relationship between wildlife and fire is more problematical. Burrowing animals survive in their insulated, underground homes while most birds and larger mammals take flight. However, less mobile creatures confined to nests, including many reptiles, insects, insect larvae, rabbits and bird hatchlings, are killed in large numbers.

*With nutrients recycled and competition removed, prairie grasses (this page) recover quickly after a fire. Fire may be an inconvenience to man, but is an integral part of the ecosystem of the prairie; without it forests would eventually replace the tallgrass prairie grasslands.*

# TALLGRASS PRAIRIE WILDLIFE

Many of the animals most commonly associated with prairies—prairie dogs and pronghorn to name just two—do not occur in the tallgrass prairie. In fact very few species are found exclusively in the tallgrass prairie. Two mammals that *are* unique to the tallgrass prairie are the Plains pocket gopher and Franklin's ground squirrel.

Except when young or during the mating season, the Plains pocket gopher rarely emerges from its vast, labyrinthine burrows. Their diet consists of plant roots, mainly those of grasses, which they harvest with their large front teeth. Their lips close behind their teeth, minimizing the amount of dirt they swallow. The Plains pocket gopher is so completely adapted to its insulated, subterranean existence that it will die quickly if exposed to the hot summer sun. Their main predator is the badger, an animal adapted especially to prey on burrowing animals.

With their long hard nails and powerful fore-feet, badgers are superbly adapted to digging for prey. They are low animals made more cryptic by their coat of the color of drying grass. They eat nearly any prey that runs, crawls or creeps.

The Franklin's ground squirrel is also a burrower, but feeds on the surface where it catches voles and grasshoppers. The Franklin's

ground squirrel is normally secretive but makes its presence known during mating time with a high-pitched whistle.

Where the tallgrass prairie and the forest intermingle there is a greater diversity of animal life. The fox squirrel, whose original habitat was once limited to the riverbank forests of the prairie, has thrived as agricultural acreage has increased and trees have spread.

---

*The Richardson's ground squirrel (facing page) is aptly nicknamed "the picket pin." The fox squirrel (above) is found throughout the eastern United States and is common in trees along prairie margins. Badgers (below) prey mainly on small mammals.*

# THE MIXED PRAIRIE

Along its western edge, the tallgrass prairie gives way to a broad north-south expanse dominated by grasses of medium height. This area, which occupies most of North and South Dakota, Nebraska and Kansas, as well as the central part of Oklahoma and a strip of north-central Texas, is known as the Great Plains, or mixed prairie. It marks the true transition between where trees can grow and where they cannot. Since trees were necessary for fuel, fences and buildings, early settlers considered this area uninhabitable, labeling the region the "Great American Desert", an area of "miles upon miles of miles upon miles".

Less precipitation (between fourteen and twenty-three inches), higher wind velocities and higher evaporation rates combine to makes the mixed prairie more arid than the tallgrass prairie. Although fire is still an important factor in the mixed prairie, it is not as clearly beneficial as in the tallgrass prairie. The burning may be beneficial or detrimental for the mixed prairie, depending on the time of year, weather, intensity, and regularity.

The little bluestem is the most characteristic grass of the mixed prairie, though the western wheatgrass gains dominance in some northern areas, occasionally eliminating little bluestem. Unlike the tallgrass prairie, which in summer is virtually uniform in height, the mixed prairie is more open and variable. This is due in part to the abundance of shortgrass prairie plants, such as buffalo and grama grasses.

Shrubs, such as shining sumac, occur throughout the mixed prairie. Trees occur as well, primarily along riverbanks, and include cottonwoods, willow and hackberry.

*Cottonwoods (these pages) are common stream-side, or "riparian," trees and produce an abundance of cotton-like seeds each summer.*

# MIXED PRAIRIE WILDLIFE

The mixed prairie marks the eastern edge of the domain of many grassland animals. Among its residents are prairie dogs, pronghorn, the swift fox and the bison, the animal that has historically symbolized the Great Plains.

## THE AMERICAN BISON

Bison originally ranged as far east as the Appalachians as well as the tallgrass prairie. The habitat that contained them in their largest numbers, however, was found on the Great Plains. Bison are wild cattle, related to antelope and deer. As a group, these animals are called ruminants, that is to say they are mammals that have evolved a special way of digesting grass.

Ruminants have stomachs that are divided into compartments. The first chamber, which receives the chewed grass, is called the rumen, and contains bacteria and protozoans that begin to break down the cellulose in the leaves. After several hours, the half-digested leaves are sent back up the throat as separate lumps to be chewed

a second time. Re-swallowed, the food is sent to the stomach proper, where it is further digested and the nutrients absorbed.

Prior to 1870 the numbers of bison (also known as buffalo) were legendary, with accounts of hundreds of thousands visible from even the modestly high vantage points available in the Plains countryside. Roaming herds covered fifty square miles, taking days to pass one point. These vast aggregations of bison were likely to have been assemblages of large numbers of smaller herds gathered together for seasonal movements. Estimates of total numbers of bison on the prairie prior to 1870 are mostly conjecture, but range between thirty million and seventy million.

A census thirty years later revealed fewer than 1,000 bison remained. Wild bison survived only in the swamps of northern Alberta, Canada and the mountains of Yellowstone National Park. The American bison would now be extinct were it not for the efforts of conservationists.

Bison are the largest terrestrial animals in North America. Their slow-moving bulk – the bison may measure seven foot at the shoulder and

weigh up to a ton – made them easy prey, and they were exterminated in their millions. Bison tongues were served as delicacies in eastern restaurants, and their hides used as rugs and industrial drive belts. All that remained after their carcasses had rotted was bones, which were crushed and used as fertilizer.

Before the area was fragmented by agriculture and their numbers decimated, the bison played an integral role in the ecology of the Plains. Their dung returned nutrients to the earth and their dead carcasses served as carrion or simply decomposed. Roaming bison herds would have had a significant impact on an area, rendering it virtually bare after the continuous grazing and trampling. The habit the bison had of creating bare earth clearings, or dust wallows, did additional damage. However, once the bison moved on, the areas would be overtaken by a succession of plants and animals and eventually recover.

*Free-roaming bison (facing page) occur only in Wood Buffalo National Park, Canada, and Yellowstone National Park, Wyoming. The bull bison (this page) is the largest terrestrial animal in North America, measuring up to twelve and a half feet in length.*

# THE PRONGHORN

The pronghorn is the fastest-moving of all North American terrestrial animals, and ranks among the fastest in the world. They may run at sustained speeds of up to 45 miles per hour and accelerate to 70 miles per hour for periods of up to four minutes. The pronghorn is also equipped with telescopic vision equivalent to five-power binoculars and can spot a predator from a great distance across their flat Plains home. If approached by a predator, such as a coyote, the pronghorn will communicate the danger to other members of the herd by spreading its rump fur, revealing a white patch.

But its speed and visual acuity was not to save the pronghorn from a fate that paralleled that of the bison. Pronghorns are naturally curious animals, attracted to nearly any novel movement. Therefore easily hunted, the pronghorn population dropped from more than fifty million in the early 1800s to less than 15,000 by 1915.

Pronghorn males are territorial during the mating season, winning the right to mate with females by holding large plots of land with good forage. The territorial boundaries are established by scent marks as well as from urine and feces. Dominant males allow female herds to remain in their territory and exclude all other males. Bachelor males and the dominant males from adjoining territories are a constant threat to these

units and the territorial males keep up a relentless guard. Females, who mate only once, continually try to move between the territories. Constant monitoring of the females' reproductive state and the defense of their territories against male intruders keep dominant males very busy during the mating season.

---

*The unique horns of the male (facing page), with their forward facing prongs, give the pronghorn its common name. Pronghorns give birth in May and June; the first mating results in a single fawn, while later unions produce twins (above). Below: a fawn hides in scrub.*

# THE SHORTGRASS PRAIRIE

The shortgrass prairie is the most arid of the mid-continental grasslands – in some places the annual precipitation is less than ten inches. Its western boundary is formed by the Rocky Mountains; on its eastern boundary a more vaguely defined transition zone separates it from the mixed prairie. The shortgrass prairie includes most of Montana as well as significant parts of eastern Wyoming, eastern Colorado, western Kansas, the panhandle region of Oklahoma, northern Texas and eastern New Mexico.

Shortgrass prairie vegetation is well adapted to the dryness of the region. Two grasses, the blue grama and buffalo grass, dominate. Buffalo grass is unique because it spreads by stolons, or above ground stems, rather than by the more typical below ground system other grasses use. The sparse vegetation of the shortgrass prairie makes fires far less common and extensive than in other prairie environments, hence the above ground method succeeds where elsewhere it would not.

Many shortgrass prairie plants form bristles, spiny coats that encompass their seeds. These bristles act like cactus spines and discourage foraging animals. They also act as dispersal mechanisms, becoming entangled in the fur of a passing animal which then transports the seed to a distant spot.

## PRAIRIE DOGS

A black-tailed prairie dog town or colony is a complicated subterranean society that may cover more than one-hundred acres and have several thousand residents. Colonies are subdivided into "wards" of from five to ten acres that usually occur between natural boundaries, such as streams and gullies. The wards are further subdivided into social groups, or "coteries", composed of up to thirty prairie dogs.

Black-tailed prairie dogs prefer areas of shortgrass which provide views over a long distance in all directions. Because their grazing is so intense, they tend the vegetation within the town with great care. When one area of town is overgrazed they move to a different part of their territory, allowing the old pasture to recover. They also cultivate selectively, cutting down seedlings of some plants to allow more room for the plants they prefer.

Natural predators of prairie dogs include coyotes, badgers, bobcats, black-footed ferrets, prairie rattlesnakes and hawks. Because they graze above ground during the day, prairie dogs have developed elaborate defenses based on their highly organized social system.

While town members are active, sentinels perched on cone shaped piles of dirt, which vary

*Black-tailed prairie dogs (below) are among the most gregarious of all mammals, engaging in "kissing," mutual grooming and cooperative burrow construction. The white-tailed prairie dog (facing page) is found in the higher elevation prairies of Wyoming, Colorado and Utah. Bottom: Big Bend National Park.*

from one to three feet high and from two to ten feet wide, watch diligently, barking and flicking their tails when danger approaches. When the alarm is sounded the animals closest to the disturbance disappear underground while those at some distance retreat to their mounds to repeat the barking call, sending the alarm rippling throughout the colony.

Eventually, when the danger has passed, the dogs will cautiously re-emerge. If all is well an "all clear" call is sounded and the colony resumes its normal activities, such as eating grasses, tending to mounds, grooming each other and resting.

As recently as the turn of the century, the number of prairie dogs residing in the mid-continental shortgrass prairies was all but incalculable. One report described a prairie dog town in Texas that contained an estimated 400 million prairie dogs and covered an area of 25,000 square miles – larger than the combined area of the states of Rhode Island, Connecticut, Massachusetts and New Hampshire. But prairie dog towns are fueled by grass, of course, which puts them in direct competition with livestock. One calculation held that 256 prairie dogs consumed as much grass as one cow and just 32 prairie dogs ate the equivalent of one sheep. Like so many other plains species, prairie dogs lost their battle for grazing rights to domestic livestock.

Assisted by the United States government, ranchers eradicated prairie dog towns using poisons and other chemicals. Their efforts were so effective that in the eastern plains the black-tailed prairie dog population dropped to an estimated ten percent of its former size. Nowadays it is largely restricted to refuges and parks. Inevitably, animals that depended on prairie dogs as prey or for habitat suffered as well. In 1980 one prairie dog predator, the black-footed ferret, was considered to be extinct, a casualty of dwindling numbers of prairie dogs and an incidental victim of poisoning.

*The black-tailed prairie dog (facing page), with its powerful front legs and sturdy claws, is well adapted to its subterranean lifestyle. Below: an alert white-tailed prairie dog acts as sentry at a burrow entrance.*

# THE BLACK-FOOTED FERRET

Until 1981, when one was killed by a ranchers dog in northwestern Wyoming, the black-footed ferret was presumed extinct. This prairie-dweller lives on a special kind of diet – the prairie dog – and requires large numbers of them to exist. They have probably always been relatively rare, even when huge prairie dog colonies covered the Great Plains. Preying exclusively on animals often considerably larger than themselves, the black-footed ferret leads a tough life. Ferrets require large ranges for their size: about one hundred acres, within which they move on average about a mile each day.

The foothills of the Rocky Mountains in northwestern Wyoming are ideal ferret habitat, a shortgrass rangeland supporting a huge complex of white-tailed prairie dog burrows. At this time biologists determined that the ferret population, though not large, was viable, and even increasing. All was well until 1984 when plague struck the prairie dog burrows. While ferrets do not suffer from the plague, prairie dogs do and the ferret population suddenly decreased by more than fifty percent. By 1986 the adult population of ferrets was put at just fourteen. These animals were taken from the wild and a captive breeding program undertaken.

Like so many other species, the black-footed ferret's habitat has been co-opted by man. In their

*The black-footed ferret (below and facing page top) spends much of its life underground. Horned larks (facing page bottom) live in the most barren of habitats.*

natural state the Great Plains can be a precarious place to live; conditions in the exposed terrain can change very quickly with catastrophic effects on plants and animals. But the plains were such a vast area that these local events, no matter how severe, were mitigated by the sheer size of the place.

## OTHER PRAIRIE DOG TOWN INHABITANTS

Prairie dog colonies are an ideal habitat for many other prairie animals. While burrowing owls eat young prairie dogs and prairie dogs eat owl eggs, they somehow coexist, with the owls nesting and raising young within the colonies. Other ground nesters are also found among prairie dog towns, including the killdeer, mountain plover, and the horned lark.

# PRAIRIE RATTLESNAKE

Prairie rattlesnakes are only active between April and October, and restrict their activity to the coolest parts of the day during the hottest parts of the summer. They locate their prey, which includes rats, mice, gophers, squirrels, chipmunks and rabbits, by scent, detecting earth-borne vibrations and using special heat detecting organs. The heat-sensing pits of the snake are located between the nostrils and eyes and provide an infrared profile of the prey, which is killed with a lethal dose of venom administered through hollow fangs.

Prairie rattlesnakes spend the Plains' harsh winter hibernating. They emerge in the spring to set out on long distance migrations, traveling in the morning and late afternoon while hiding in holes and crevices during the hottest part of the day. These migrations often begin with the onset of severe thunder and rain storms, probably to limit their exposure to predators like eagles, hawks, coyotes, bobcats and humans. They may cover more than half a mile a day, and during the two to three week migration, travel an average of more than three miles.

In the plains of south-central Wyoming a favorite food source, the deer mouse, guides the rattlesnake migrations. When sufficient mouse odor is detected, indicating a large population, the migration is finished and the prairie rattlesnakes settle in for a summer of eating and mating. While receptive females make the migration, pregnant female prairie rattlers do not, preferring to forage nearer the wintering dens.

In response to the shorter days and falling temperatures of late August, the snakes begin the return migration to their dens. Following roughly the same route, they use the sun for orientation and may also use geographical landmarks to return to the same den they used the previous winter.

*Rattlesnakes (facing page top) have special heat-detecting organs called loreal pits with which they locate prey, and adopt an aggressive defense posture (facing page bottom) when in danger. The unfortunate deer mouse (below) is their favorite food.*

# PRAIRIE BIRDS

Ferruginous hawks will nest in trees when available, but throughout most of its range (the drier parts of the northern Great Plains) it settles for low bushes, ledges or even the ground. As with many hawks, the female stays near the nest while the male forages for both her and the nestlings. They adopt a range of strategies to catch their prey. A hawk will swoop down from great heights to catch prairie dogs or stand outside a gopher mound for hours waiting to pounce on the unsuspecting rodent. Other prey includes snakes, squirrels, meadow larks and an occasional bat.

The greater and lesser prairie chickens are similar birds, separated only by size and habitat preference. The greater prairie chicken is found in the tallgrass and mixed prairies while the smaller and paler lesser prairie chicken resides in the shortgrass prairie. Unfortunately they too are losing their habitat to farmers and, therefore, decreasing in numbers. The lesser prairie chicken is estimated to occupy only ten percent of its former range and numbers less than 40,000 birds.

The sharp-tailed grouse is a close relative to both the prairie chickens and occasionally interbreeds with the greater. With habitat requirements less specialized than either prairie chicken species, grouse have survived the conversion to farmland in much larger numbers, expanding into areas of the northern coniferous forest that have been cleared by logging.

The mating system of all three birds involves the males displaying communally on a traditional site known as a "lek." Males compete for mates with displays that involve ritualized dances and the inflation of brightly colored air sacs in their necks. Using these sacs they emit characteristic "booming" calls.

Three of North America's largest birds; the whooping crane, the sandhill crane and the trumpeter swan, were once common on the prairies. All have suffered from the draining of wetlands.

After facing imminent extinction, the whooping crane has made somewhat of a comeback. Their nesting area along the Sass River in Wood Buffalo National Park in Canada is now protected, as is their wintering ground on the salt flats of the Aransas Wildlife Refuge in Texas. Each year, however, exposed to everything from power lines to pesticides, the migration period takes its toll on the small number of birds remaining.

The smaller sandhill crane has adapted better to the advent of agriculture by switching its diet to grain. But, with estimates that a single sandhill crane can consume $3,000 worth of grain, it is in constant conflict with farmers.

Like the two cranes, trumpeter swans have been displaced from the central plains where they once nested. Hunted for their meat by early settlers and prized for their densely feathered skins, they are another example of a species driven almost to extinction.

---

*Sandhill cranes (below) have fared far better than whooping cranes, but their numbers are nevertheless decreasing due to loss of habitat. Male lesser prairie chickens (facing page top) gather and engage in communal courtship displays that include inflating their red neck flaps with air. Facing page bottom: the trumpeter swan, once in danger of extinction. Now fully protected, it has been reintroduced into parts of its former range.*

# PRAIRIE POTHOLES

Even the most arid regions of the Great Plains offer more than just miles of featureless grass and farmland. Major portions of Montana, North and South Dakota, Minnesota and Iowa include a unique remnant of the ice age, a wetland marsh known as the prairie pothole. The pothole region extends northward into the Canadian states of Saskatchewan, Manitoba and Alberta, where most of North America's waterfowl breed. Largely destroyed by agricultural plowing in the United States, potholes account for just a small fraction of wetlands, but contribute up to one half of the waterfowl production.

Prairie potholes are clay-lined low spots which were left when the ice sheet retreated 10,000 years ago. They trap and hold water from the spring thaw, supporting a full range of marsh plants, including cattails, bulrushes and water lilies. Following the wholesale destruction of prairie pothole wetlands, waterfowl numbers have crashed. Pintails, blue-winged teal, mallards, scaup, wigeon, redheads, and canvasbacks have all been affected. The estimated numbers of ducks decreased by nearly forty percent between 1969 and 1988. Most of the surviving potholes, a third of the nations remaining supply, are found in North Dakota. There has been a concerted effort, both from private organizations and the United States government, to restore some of this waterfowl habitat lost to agriculture.

*Above right: wildflowers surround a prairie pothole. North America's duck populations depend on these pothole wetlands to breed, and their conversion for the purposes of agriculture has led to a steady decline in the number of ducks. Canvasbacks (right) are diving ducks, propelling themselves underwater with large feet on short legs set far back on their bodies. The American wigeon (center right) is a dabbling duck. Dabblers skim food from the surface of the water or feed in the shallows by tipping forward and submerging their heads and necks. Like most other ducks, mallards (far right) perform their courtship on the surface of the water. They are monogamous for a season, changing mates each year.*

# A TALE OF THREE DOGS

The wholesale changes to Americas mid-section have resulted in many wildlife fatalities, mostly due to shrinking habitats. There have also been occasional winners; some animals have taken advantage of the change to farmland and ranching to increase their range and numbers.

Wolves, the largest of the North American canids, were once common on the Great Plains, preying on the vast bison herds. Hunted and poisoned, they have nearly been eliminated from the lower forty-eight states. In contrast, at a mere five pounds in weight, the swift fox is the smallest of all North American canids. Historically the swift fox was common throughout the shortgrass and mixed grass prairies of the Great Plains. By 1900, however, it was rare, an incidental victim of the settlers' war against the wolf.

In the Great Plains a common way to kill wolves was to lace undevoured bison carcasses with poison. Probably because they did not consider them serious competitors, wolves paid little attention to the tiny swift foxes which were often the first to take the poison. However, wolves *did* consider coyotes significant competitors and kept

*Black-tailed prairie dogs (above) have lost ninety percent of their population, due mainly to domestic cattle ranching. Loathed by the ranchers, wolves (below) are condemned to extinction by law in several Prairie states. Facing page: exploitation of North America's grasslands climaxed with the Dust Bowl of the 1930s. After wind-blown soil had darkened the sky from coast to coast, grassland conservation legislation was enacted. Overleaf: bison roam freely in Yellowstone National Park's Haden Valley.*

them considerably below their current levels. By 1890 the wolf was gone, the adaptable coyote had proliferated and the prairie largely converted to farmland. The swift fox was in trouble, its young a favorite food of the coyote.

Without man's help, the swift fox was losing its battle for survival. The species is now protected in several states and a captive breeding and reintroduction program has reintroduced them to the Canadian provinces of Alberta, Saskatchewan and Manitoba. Without the wolf to keep the coyote in check and with the prairie itself far less extensive than it used to be, the fox, although increasing in numbers, will require constant scrutiny.

Though the wolf, grizzly bear, wolverine and puma have been eliminated from the Plains, the coyote remains. Like the others it has been trapped, shot, poisoned and hunted, but despite this ordeal its range has increased. The coyote survives because it is so adaptable, eating just about anything. They hunt effectively in pairs, often with one flushing the unsuspecting prey into the jaws of the other. They are also prolific, raising six or seven pups at a time, and have become progressively more wary of poison.

# PRAIRIE CONSERVATION

Nearly all the American prairie is gone, converted to farm and ranchland. The area that once made up the tallgrass prairie is still easily identified, replaced as it is almost entirely by corn, which thrives there without irrigation. Winter wheat, along with cattle and sheep, identify the areas where the vast herds of bison once roamed and prairie dogs built huge towns.

The changes are irreversible; this area is the "bread basket" to an ever increasing human population that needs to eat. Much of the change occurred in an era when the continent seemed endless. Millions of acres of the prairie were used as marginal farmland and, once abandoned, its topsoil washed into the sea.

Few could have imagined that countless million of bison would be reduced to 600 in so few years. While there is simply no room nowadays for the majestic herds of the 1800s, the bison population has recovered significantly. Over 60,000 can be found in national parks and private preserves today. Because pronghorn eat different plants than cattle, ranchers tolerate them and their recovery has been even more dramatic.